When Hard Times Seep Through To Your Soul

A book of Poetry for the struggle along the journey

KREATIVITY

authorHOUSE®

AuthorHouse™
1663 Liberty Drive
Bloomington, IN 47403
www.authorhouse.com
Phone: 1-800-839-8640

First published by AuthorHouse 6/2/2010

ISBN: 978-1-4490-8658-9 (sc)

Library of Congress Control Number: 2010907865

Printed in the United States of America
Bloomington, Indiana

This book is printed on acid-free paper.

To Chalina Howell-Trent who though she has been the cause of many of the most turbulent and tramadic moments in my life; she's more importantly been the cause of all of the happiest ones

About The Author

Keith Trent was lovingly brought into this world at Brookdale Hospital to Alan and Sheryl Trent on August 8th 1982. From an early age he showed the will to be a performer. Growing up Keith and his family members would put on shows and entertain the rest of the family. Keith was always very creative and even in his earliest years in school began showing that. At around only the second or third grade he excelled at telling stories and even created comic books at home. As well as wrote his earliest and most basic poems. By the fifth grade Keith was writing mysteries and selling them during lunch at school. However when Keith got to the seventh grade he discovered his new favorite thing in life... basketball. Keith began to pour everything he had into teaching himself how to play and excelling in the sport despite fierce ridicule and opposition. His ultimate goal was to become a basketball player. However when he got to High School and eventually the tenth grade he met a girl who sparked his love of poetry again. He was so inspired he wrote a book of fifty poems in three days. Thus his love for poetry was reborn. Over the years Keith continued to build his craft often using poetry to try to woo the girls of his dreams though his poetry seemed more effective when borrowed by others than used by himself. Though due to many constant injuries Keith had to give up his dream of the NBA he discovered his purpose in Acting. Over the last thirteen years Keith has worked tirelessly to achieve his goal of a substantial and fulfilling career in film and television but has never lost his will to write. After spending lots of time in poetry jams during his college years Keith has recently rekindled his love for that world. Always admiring the spoken word format of poetry Keith was determined to learn and excel in this style. Through much time, practice, and study Keith was prepared for what lied ahead at his new Spoken Word home, Soule Restaurant, in Brooklyn NY. Keith met Justinah Mcfadden otherwise known as Poetic Justice and was inspired by her vision and insightfulness. As well as the many other phenomenal poets he has befriended there. He then decided to collaborate with Justinah under her company, Collection Of Thoughts, to achieve one of his longest dreams. To have his poetry immortalized in print for the whole world to finally see.

Introduction

When hard times seep through to your soul is a book that is very close to my heart. Growing up in a loving and Christian two parent home people can tend to think you're life is perfect. In my case that is very far from the truth. Though I grew up in a very positive environment the world had plenty of terrible experiences to share with me over the years. I have nearly died in multiple car crashes. I have had my life physically threatened on one too many occasions. I have excelled and pushed through with extreme determination in many jobs and in my purpose as an actor and writer only to be thoroughly betrayed and defeated. And last but not least have suffered some of the most tragic and tumultuous relationships a man of my caliber of love can imagine. Through all of these experiences God has kept me whole. When everything around me crumbled time and time again I could always depend on his foundation still standing unscathed beneath my feet. That is the essence of this book. I have written many pieces in the past as well as recently expressing my ups, my downs, my trails, tribulations, and turmoil. I have chronicled the pain, the hurt, the rage, the cries; toward God as well as the world. However what the book in totality embodies is a perpetual spirit of hope. Sustained in my faith in Jesus Christ. That screams no matter how much pain, no matter how much despair, in the end I will not be broken because the victory is already won. So, laugh with me, cry with me, ponder the ways of the world and love with me, and explore what happens when hard times seep through to the soul.

Soon to come...

The Walk Of Love

For Further Info
Contact Author at:

Ketrent@msn.com

Table Of Contents

When Hard Times Seep Through To Your Soul

Cycle Of A Tortured Soul

Frustration, Boredom, Anger, Desperation, Anxiety, Helplessness, Rage, On the verge, Of Snapping, Breaking, Cracking, Bubbling up, About to Explode, Agony, Torture, Pain, Flowing, disappointment, Confusion, Disarray, Lost, Wishful, Hopeful, Feels like not enough, Emotional, Panicking, Want to, Scream, Out loud, Start a fight, Hurt, Let go, Of peace, Of joy, Curse, Do wrong, Spiraling, Downward, Crashing, Can't handle, Can't bear, On my own, But he can, Reverse all, Negative, done?

The Myth

Hello ladies and gentleman
I'm a myth
I don't exist
Least that's what I got u tellin yourself
I'm the master of lies
I mean revealer of truth
Got control of humanities lives
Yeah I'm that sly
Screw the other guy
With his rules morality and holiness
Cause I let you do what you want
You only live once right
So u might as well do everything
Long as it makes feel good
On the outside
Man I'm nice
I'm just a tale to scare you
Says the puppet on a string
Your the maker of your own destiny
Yet I manipulate your everything
Liberal=servant to my anarchy
Humanities submission to my humanity
Free of the restrictions of him
Kindredness to the flames
Of my legacy
Free to be me
Oh I even got niggas kissin each other
Thugged out or not
Marriages endin 50% of the time
Dudes and chicks
Turnin to pimps and hos
People sleepin with anything wearin clothes
Preteens even feenin on addiction
To alcohol n drugs
Forget young thugs
Babies are havin babies
With no daddy or no mama
Yeah I'm no actor but I sure bring the drama

Thank you for all those who made me a myth
How much easier to rule when you no longer exist
But thanks even more for the forgetting of him
And even more to his believers for so frequently compromising
I've been called so many names
Like Lucifer and Devil
But thanks for the new title
Of non existent emperor
So please continue to ignore me
And keep on living your lives

The Devils Cry

You may not like me
But you will get to know me
Cause I'll always be standing over you
Looming over you
Screaming in your ear
Until you crack
Because I hate, despise, disgust, loathe you
I won't stop until you are all destroyed
No matter how strong you get
No matter how many times you succeed
I'll never go away until I gain my throne
I'll wait until your guard is down
I'll prey on you insecurities
You will fall
Oh please believe
So never feel free enough to sleep
Cause I won't

I catch myself reciting cynical lines
I've lost my positive vibe
Cause I've been disappointed too many times
Don't bother with hope for the best
Just prepare for the rest
And if something good happens
Never get set in happiness
Chances are a catastrophes lurking around the bend
So enjoy it while it lasts
But anticipate the swift end
Plunging you into turmoil again
These are the thoughts that fill my head
My mind recalls words like hope and faith
But they no longer hold a firm place
Within my brain
Joyful moments no longer feel the same
When you can constantly feel the lurking pain
Like rain drops harshly crashing against window panes
Or the shrill screeching of halting trains
I've been paralyzed by the looping cycle of tragic ends
When will it end
The sons love be felt again
When will revelation translate further than just this pen
When will I experience victory over more than sin
More than victory over death
In a way that makes this life feel worth living

You're like my identical twin
You body
Me spirit within
You temptin me to sin
Constantly
Me clingin to Christ
Tryin to break free
Of this evil humanity
Tryin to separate me from eternity
With him
This long time battle of epic proportion is
The only war that really matters
The battle for my spirits final resting place
With Jesus safe forever
Or eternally doomed for trustin in myself
Or others
Like Adam did
Spiralin us into the longest losin streak in history
And after 2000 yrs of guaranteed victory
We still gotta be thoroughly convinced to leave the losin team
Even those who live as best they can for him
Toil hard to avoid multiple stints of sin
In which we feel embarassin
And even when forgiven
Struggle to escape the shame within
Though he made so many promises
We feel we've to badly compromised on them
Lived so many days doubtin them
Due to so many harsh realities lived with him
In your heart
When you thought that meant heaven would start
On earth
But heavens on another plain
And he said you must die daily for him
Which means in the end we will become his diamonds
But right now we must endure the rough
Cause after our trial by fire on these so temporary grounds
He's promised we'll never see fires true face
Destined for those who didn't believe he ever existed
Or sent his son Jesus to die for their sins

Yes all our sins will also be counted
But our repentant hearts
Resulting from his transformation
Will entitle us to his destined plane of existence
For us his chosen children
In that he knew before time tilted in his direction forward
That we would ultimately never go back
To the ways of Adam if it were within our will
Cause we would resubmit our spirits back to his will
And be in one accord once again
On a new earth similar to Eden
With God

They say when you love what you do
You'll never work a day in your life
But I guarantee you that was said by a rich man
Not a three jobs just to squeak by for your family man
Or a non English speaking bottom of the barrel jobs immigrant
Scratching to the base of their nails for the crumbs left of the
American dream hustla man
Scorned by the leaders of the government
Givin up their lives for their children man
Dignity ain't worth empty bellies for his wife and children
Broken dreams and sleepless nights to him are worth all his sufferin
It's sickenin
We may finally have got a black president
But trust the dark and brown are surely still strugglin
And Americas still workin hard to exile the immigrant
Although he's one too and we the ones responsible for establishin him
And all his friends seemingly monopolizin successfulness
Unless they sell a brutha an advance and a dream
So he can floss all day while you steal all his cream
But there are a select few
Who are tamed before the shrew
Who put their art ahead of the jewels
And are somehow able to support their family too
I know, I just wanna be
I just wanna be successful
But this glass seems to be less than half full
So from Christ's strength I try to pull
But these years are getting long
More than a decade has passed
And I'm still singin that song
Now years of shunned doubts
Are saying you've been forewarned
The demons charged with my demise
No longer need to disguise
They dance and jump so high
They appear reclaim the sky
But I sit and I think
Will I achieve the status of the few
Or resign to the demise
Of the broken and destitute

Can I achieve true purpose
Not just in heaven but on earth too
And multiply the talents
Like God intended me to do
Honoring those who lost and gave so much so that I wouldn't have to
See I keep chasin elusive dreams
Cause their nightmares eternally
Keep me from complacent sleep
So I spurn scheme after scheme
Cause I'm incapable of non-belief
That this isn't what Jesus has intended for me
I know they say that success is the key
But my successes they seem so rudimentary
To the catastrophic chemistry
Of what I want my career to be
So dismal to the expanse
My desire burns inside for my destiny
It's almost as if the shear massiveness of my goals
Is crushin me
Collapsin me
So airs so thin
That I can't breathe
I scream for God to validate me
So I don't fall from these epic heights of inadequacy
Into the pits of looming failures finality
Into the abyss of broken dreams
The Casams where hasbeens and giver uppers
Go to die
Where cynics and critics thrive
And haters always win
The place where Satan no longer needs sin
Cause he's already got your purpose captive
Should I "rise" like a helium balloon
Full of hot air
Live a life full of regrets and despair
Live an ordinary life
And just roll with the punches
Pay bills on time
Live to just die
And then in heaven reside

Leavin no legacy on earth behind
And fade away from existence
Leaving no true marks on the minds
Of anyone
Or will I do more then just write and recite lines
Accomplishing all my purest desires
With the gifts the lord designed to provide
His stories in the books of all mankind
Well your guess is as good as mine
But one thing is sure
Imma try till I die
Or till it kills me first
Cause giving up is incompressible
To this man of rebirth

These burdens of responsibilities
Seem beyond my means
Above my reach
Make me just wanna
SCREAM!!!!!!!!!!
Dignity of dreams
Seemingly decreed
To be killed by defeat
Poisoned by the disease
Of irrational inadequacy
Why me
Skill plus desire
Would reasonably equal victory
But apparently not in the world of me
How much passion
How much desire is required
How many tools must be acquired
To reach achieved instead of inspired
How many tears must I expire
To happy days retire
Cause I'm tired... of this despair
I want more than my conscience clear
Cause I'm more than aware
That life is just not fair
But blessings are supposed
To rain on me too
As well as the unjust
On these principles I trust
So where's my cut
I extend myself as much
I give of love
I control my lusts
How much is enough
I don't pretend to a perfect human be
I just ask more often to my positive harvest reap

I see him and I cower
Every variation of him
Sends chills thru my skin
Cause I feel a sacredness of kin within
Like just one more wrong choice
One more wrong turn
One more misfortune
And I'll be right beside him
Singin the same sad song
Quoting the same sad words
The speeches of the scorned
Holding the signs of his dying world
The stench of his fallen dreams
Feeling the gaping hole of the presence of his preserving angels
Where his demons now stretch their wings
Stinking of iniquity
Sin vomited from choked on hopelessness
Despair lurking in his surly breathed air
The brokenness in his eyes screams at me from their gaze as they reach
mine
And I can't help but lower my head
Fighting the spirits that are trying to latch themselves to me
They would love to see my talent to end up this way
Running mazes through the streets
Raped of its true blessings
Where very few will see
Except the others like the now me
Still dreamers
Not unrealized potential lining streets
In poverty
Not always clearly destitute reminders
Of how little pure talent can really mean
In this cold world of public schemes
And broken dreams
Where struggles smile on kind faces
And tears cry on the elegantly played and sung songs of the talented
poor
We appease with our merest pennies everyday

I entrusted you with my soul
I supported you behind every fall
In you I placed my all
And you repaid me by crushing my goals

What was the point
Of entrusting you my heart
If you knew you never had my back
Right from the start

You cried for me to hold on
Yet you only breed in me scorn
You lied to draw me in
Then made your home under my skin

You were such a part of me
You were contagious to the touch
Because of me you were fed to others too
So much so they still come to me to beg for food

But when I need to eat
They never seem in reach
Just left me starved n empty
Tryin not to feel incomplete

Your ways through me often made them feel whole
But often left me feeling drained and old
Unsuccessful in my goals
Burdened once again to fall

You said to trust in you
And you'd never do me wrong
But though others seem to get lucky
When I help renew their belief in you
For me you never seem to come through

My victories pale in comparison
To the exploits that others do
And I'm not beggin for mans glory
Just my portions due

Cause unlike sin
I thought u faith would feed off gratitude
The magnitude in which I try to do right
Not perfect but a willing sacrifice
Dyin daily to live like Christ
Mistakes I might
Cause I'm entrapped in human plight
But damn it I do fight
Whole heartedly day till night
To shine through the dark his light
Though not worthy of his sight
So why, faith, do you abuse me so with your denial

When does talent turn to prosperity
Faith into fulfilled promises
Trials and tribulations
To success
Or am I just holding my breath
Or are these feats impossible
Is pain and hurt
All this world is full of
Disappointments all I'm destined for
Talent meant for amusement for a lucky some
But for me purely troublesome
Devoid of usefulness
Accept as a mere torture
For a miserable wretch like me
Will darkness be all I ever see
With only pointless glimpses of the heavenly
Till I'm desperate enough to put a premature end to this tragedy
To just give up on old and happily
Lay down my life
Filled primarily with sin and strife
Hand my soul and spirit
Into the hands of the deceiver
Bow cowardly to the Devil
And resign myself to the eternal flames
Even though Christ overcame
Torture beyond what my mind can comprehend as pain
Just turn my back on him again
Engulfed in my own dismay
Or do I wipe the defeat from my eyes
And rise
Do I stand on his word divine
Do I submit my all to him
My essence my spirit his gifts
My abilities my talents
The things he's perfected within
And allow him to bend them to his will
And trust in his time his promises he'll
Fulfill

We can't let these niggers get too big

That's the words that dwell within
This worlds winds

They may blow softer and more subtle than earlier days
But they surely do remain...
They spoon feed u fame
Till your stuffed fat with this worlds praise...
Then they back stab
And kick from risen heights
They soar circles like buzzards over your accomplishments
They pick at human cracks
Hoping to your humanity crack
And lie in wait to report the damage

Worldwide news
The fall was greater than the rise
Why support hard work and drive

Why try to duplicate
When you can just sling hate
How bout some degrading names...
False accusations
Criticisms overflowing with rage
All this and all you really know is a name
Not a person but you don't care
They have all you've never made
They've also endured more than you've even tried
Even childhood innocence denied
All for goals and dreams to strive

Built others pockets up
On their backs many ride
And often it's not enough
Their only humans too but tough

How dare they succeed farther than I
How dare they excel and thrive
Me I'd rather criticize

Hipocritize
Mastermind your demise
This is what the world cries

Well I'll overcome
I'll overshadow tales of past times
I'll give more than blood sweat and tears till I die
I'll submit my goals my dreams my purpose to Christ
And for him I'll live my life
Falls and short comings he'll push aside
With forgiveness
Since in his strength I'll thrive
And in his mercy and glory abide

After all our ancestors went thru
Niggas still hittin stages like coons
Then have the stones to call themselves artists
But where is the art
All I see is the masters piece
Aimed at your feet while your still
Pastime tap dancin
So I don't buy into what this new generation is sellin
I don't conform to this worlds ways
Imma try my best to step on the stage
With Christ's true creativity
Which he destined me intuitively
Infusing it internally
Purposing me eternally
So despite minor setbacks
The devil could never break me majorily
So I could influence Gods integrity
Into this worlds perversity
Of an industry intended for his ministry
So though I'm also not worthy
My humility would give him the Glory
As I would wholeheartedly try to not go astray
Yet be willing to have him put all my fallen crookeds straight
While I walk his straight n narrow

Niggas are linin our streets
As chalk lines
What ever happened to the African American dream
Corners are screaming from the blood of our people
Running through their drains
Where all our peoples iniquities take place
When will we rise from corners to the rooftops of buildings
From niggas to black
Trade Gods word for straps
Grasp the true weapons
He destined for his glory
In his victory
Over death an sin
For us

THUG

Triflin
Homicidal
Underachievin
Gangsta
And I know we're outta letters
But ignorant
And this is what the ladies want
Cause he's a man that takes control
Yeah of your life
His terms of endearment
Are shawty, trick, and ho
He's tricked you into imprisonment
With baby daddy antics
Or strikes across the face
But you just needed a taste
Of that brutha that makes others tremble
Cause that's just so sexy
Till he's terrorizin you n your babies
Stranglin any hope for peace
Now you wish you could erase his exterior
Be with someone who doesn't treat you as inferior
But now this beast has grabbed hold of you
And the only way he plans on lettin you leave is in a bag

PSA

I just wanna start by letting you know this ain't no G rated poem
Now that we've got that out of the way
I've got a very urgent PSA
That's Public Service announcement
For those unfamiliar with the abbreviation
We live in a nation where older
"Negros" find themselves dislikened to the word Nigga
This unrest is due to the fact that yes; white people created this old
And hateful word
And frustration has arisen
Due to the youth's reconstruction
And subsequent constant re use
Well for the aged
Slavery is over
Last time I checked wasn't nobody physically in chains lately unless
they got they black tails arrested
Now before you exhume your anger and commence to air me your frustrations
Yes
I agree
The youth
Are way to comfortable with its use
But frankly how much more important is it that
NIGGERS
STILL
EXIST
Screw the kids who use it too often to say my friend
How about your anger to the black dude that put his gun to your head
And said empty out your wallet
The black dudes that make you sometimes even subconsciously cross the
street in your own damn neighborhood
The black dude tryna sell drugs to you n your kids because they're too lazy to
get a real damn job and earn money the hard but right way
Or the African American who knows nothing of his background or his
ancestors struggles and could care less
The Negro satisfied with livin off the government
The smelly bum who would rather drink away every pilfered penny
rather than in a suit invest
The corrupt cop that falsely incarcerates or kills his own brothers

unjustly to fit in with the white man
The snob who looks down on his brother
The group that jumps one or the few
The dad who's face we don't see so his boy must become the man
The never doer but always the fan
The people who unite for colors and turf because they've no real fam
The orphan practically slaughtered like the lamb
The niggers that strike fear in the hearts of the mass
The reason you might not get the chance
The reason people when your close grab their bags
Yeah we finally got one president
But when will we lay off the kids for using a word and focus more on
the people that are it
The realest truest enemy of the black man
The livin Nigger

Ghetto
And loud as hell
Gold teeth in her mouth
And looks you couldn't sell
I don't know what's worse
Her sloppy frame
Or the spewing of ignorance that leaks to mouth from brain
A sad case rather than lady
To her kids she's a shame
Hitting the club at 40 with her daughters as her friends
Smoked away role model for bad example in exchange
She needs holy intervention on top of prayers
But she turns that all away
Trapped in this destructive mindset
Slave to her own inability to expand her thought process
The hood is not in her head its seeped in and saturated her spirit
Causing all her actions to seem deplorable n desperate
They seem to make all the stereotypes seem true
With ignorance and stupidity synonymous with black skin hue
And all I can do is shake my head
Not with contempt but with pity
And honestly pray that one day she'll let Jesus in and wipe her soul
clean from sin
Allowing her mind to transcend
Before she realizes that there really is no ghetto for those whose
destiny is heaven in the end

We send them back in hoards
But what do they come here for
Rarely for their health
For fun to steal our jobs
Or take over our country
But because of their most basic desires
To support their ailing families
Were lazy and they don't have any time for greed
So they leave everything they know
They buck against more than just the system
They often even give up most of their culture
Necessities drive them
Not the luxuries we Americans
And I use the term loosely
Cause despite appearances sake
How American can an African really get
But I digress
Not the luxuries we Americans sell our souls for
Forget Jesus we want quick fortune and fame without any hard work
Yet those who exhibit it we disgrace
And we complain and we extricate
They're stealing our unwanted jobs!
They're overcrowding our streets!
Yet we sell the world the ideal
Of our holy American Dream
But it's just becoming a glorified Sodom n Gomorrah filled with gross
iniquities
Yet we're judge and jury
And executioner/extricator of the whole entire universe
My country tis of thee
Sweet land of liberty
Of thee I see
Please

Pull Your Damn Pants Up

Does anybody like to see the behind of a young man
Just by a show of hands
Didn't think so
So if I may suggest
Men pull up your damn pants
I mean last time I checked underwear was meant
To go UNDER what you wear
And I don't know if this bothers anyone but me
But since when are pants supposed to hang below your knees
It's just another case of mistaken identity
Cause last time I checked this trend began in the penitentiary
So I don't know who thought it cool to bring to the streets
What prison guards did so inmates wouldn't use belts for assisted
suicides
Besides you look like a friggin idiot wadlin like a penguin
Cuttin of the circulation
To your hips and your thighs
Why do you insist on hangin them low
Like chains I hate that even more
Got your jeans draggin on the floor
And you still got a belt on
If I can see your entire boxers
Why'd you bother wearing your jeans at all
Why aren't we picketing the streets
This is a new age travesty
Is no one else as disgusted as me
I know in these times this may seem an unlikely issue to write a poem
about
But I'm tired of seeing exposed backsides everywhere I go
So join the cause and tell the next fool you see with his ankle pants
on
Pull your damn pants up

Fame

You have constantly eluded me
Left me many nights without sleep
Sitting up for hours
Trying not to weep
I give you my all to achieve
But it appears that you want more of me
And I say I'll abstain
I know now
All you want to do is stain
You want my allegiance to his campaign
Well I'd rather endure this pain
The pain of the hard way
I'll sleep much better without regret
My soul you will never get
For you I'll make no blood sacrifice
No one will lose their life
Christ already paid the price
Up on that cross
No one will die for my ascension
Cause he already died for my ascension
No more Tupacs'
No more Biggies'
No more Aaliyahs'
No more sons, brothers, sisters, mothers
Will die in vain
My soul
You will never capitalize on its pain
I will endure for the almighty
I will hold on to his integrity
If you must allude me forever
So shall it be
Because there is only one deity
The one who gave these gifts to me
I am not confused
I will not commit abominations in your name
Become slave to unnatural behaviors
To comply with sick pale male desires
Illuminati will never rape my soul or my body

Free your masons if you please
I'm immune to your disease
I have only one to please
I only pray upon these knees
That he will have mercy on your followers
And that their unwitting followers will one day see the truth
Before it's too late
And fame has had its way
With their soul
And they try to cleanse it with drugs and alcohol
Only to meet fames final resting place
Satan's final resting place
The flames
And they become the flaming
Coincidental no it's foreshadowing
This body is only for borrowing
So I no longer want to be famous
I want to be known
For committing my art to him
Standing on his promises
Whether or not it leads to riches
Cause I kept my eye on heavens riches
And trust I'll reap what I sow

False images flow up and down matrix screens
Unplug yourself from the lies of normalcy
No one aspires to be a great human anymore
The industry is filled with gods
Not ruled by boundaries or morals
Yet it's them who garnishes the highest praise
How many truly know Jesus
How many even care
As long as they get the money
The money and the cars
Cars n the clothes
The ho's
I suppose
I'd rather be drugged and loved
Till I become too unstable and have to get snubbed
Addicts have to start somewhere
So a failure I am dubbed
Don't worry tomorrow the industry
Will shuffle out a new one
And you'll forget the industry was addiction number one
Cause now your having fun
You'll never even realize when the pattern hits repeat
The "entourage" traditionally enablers pacify you to defeat
So another can rise to the peak
Continuing the aspirations
Ignoring all the lost ones
Overlooking all the coincidental tragedies
Ignoring the steadily growing signs
That no longer feel the need to even hide no more
Cause you'll defend them till your brain washed stains
Leak onto your own misguided misfortunes
You'll never acknowledge the soul
Has been sold in exchange
Cause fortune and fame
Hold the blind fold of His scheme
The well thought out plan
To desensitize the world to His true reign
Illuminati only think they hold the reins
But all their money and power is in vain
Cause they'll only join Him in the eternal flames

And He'll have one last laugh in the end
Cause He knows best no matter how hard He's tried to fight it since He
denied His own purpose for His own creation
That there is only one creator
One alpha and omega
One true master
Only one being that truly is God
And he doesn't force anyone to walk the footsteps he's placed for you
So which one will you choose

Imma do this
And imma do that
Alot of people be on that chitter chat
But do they really got your back
They're never found on the follow through
I be on that imma do what I gotta do
The most realistic attitude
Is I'll believe it when I see it
Cause I just don't have the time to wait on u

We Call It Higher Learning but is it
In a system constantly stained with the stupidity of politicians
What could be rich and productive is
Raped of its true virtue
Your so called education no longer interests me
It bores and disgusts me
The foolishness you call intelligence
Urks me to the very core of my soul
You drain me of my energy
And cage my soaring creativity
It's appalling you consider this needed
To strip away my desire to live
With these arrogant, self gratifying teachers
Forcing their own moronic views on me
Charge outrageous tuition fees
To fund wars that could end my life
Your education is an abomination
And I will not allow it to destroy
The eagles of purpose and creativity
Yearning to fly free
You will never cage me
In your abysmal black hole abyss
Called Higher learning

Four Walls

I spent so many years behind those
Four walls
So I would never be forced into your box
Average I am not
Cause I held the stars in my imaginations eyes early
I never intended to be contained by your gravity
I'm more than the crab in me
My nails don't scrape no pans or pots
Cause I've transcended your meager plain
So I also don't grab at supposed to be liberated chains
So you too can share my pain
I only hold onto him
On him I cast all my doubts and my fears
So that the road to ultimate success is clear
But I am only human
I too am wrapped in rebellious skin
Sacred kin to him that seeks to destroy me
I feel lust for power and desires as well
But I fight the enemy that was born inside me
Thought innocent infant
Yet inherited baby sin
Once sin was my suckled baba
Now I take comfort in aba fatha
I matured early puttin my dreams
In his purpose for stability
And then I pushed wholeheartedly
Vowing only death could stop me
While claiming Christ's will proudly
Darin anyone to doubt me
Cause my resolve couldn't be soundless
Cause his victories reach was boundless
Cause his unconditional love is endless
So though so many years have past
And my dreams are still in route
Instead of doubt
I get on my knees in these four walls instead
Cause church overrules college
In a spiritual mindset
Cause my creativity could never fit

Will never submit
To the claustrophobic four walls
Of your cubicle death

Feeling like a Negro
Waiting to enter my own performance through the
back door
I am in a cramped space
I'm tired n hungry
And my drive seems insignificant
In comparison to my status
In modern day segregation
Futuristic degradation
I'm non union
People are getting rich and famous off of reality t.v.
People are music and movie stars
With far less talent then we
They don't even slightly resemble the level
That God has gifted me
And if they do they're blowin it through
Addiction to all types of forms of promiscuity
And all I want is to feed my need
To fulfill my purpose through my craft
And feed my family
Yet my chances are so limited
I'm starting at a handicap
I look around in this cramped cave
For non members
While the members live in style
Like heathens gazing at heaven from hell
And I can't help but feel
Can my talent overcome
Or will I be engulfed by the sum
The elite
Not even be able to spread my wings
Die stifled with my Kreativity
A victim
To the system
The actors union

Backslidin

I know we all start on the bottom
But so many slowly raise to the top
Finding strength in your footsteps
Submitting themselves to you
And I did so too
But like so many among the few
I've reached a place where I can't feel u
I say prayers in your name
Set goals for myself in vain
Feel like I'm eroding from all this pain
Falling back into sin once again
Why do I turn away from you
Let this skin lure me into sin
Cleanse myself of filthy mistakes
Only to repeat them over again
Why do I continue this pattern
That destroys my soul within
I've screamed at you
Asked what you want me to do
Like I don't owe my
My everything to you
I know Christ died so of my sin I'm free
So why is it's hold so strong over me
So fleeting seem all my victories
This monster so hard to remove from me
I'm headed toward some terrible tragedy
If I can't overcome this humanity
And stop my backsliding
To elevate my soul to the Christ in me
My brother and sister please pray with me

Perfect Design

Homo
Faggot
Queer
Queen
Puff
Transgender
Gay
Confused
Misguided
Abomination
This is what they call you
They want to cleanse the earth of you
At times I've found myself caught up too
But this is not what God intended for you
You're not exclusive to breaking his strict rules
We all fall short of the Glory of God
This is not something we can overcome
On our own
Though we try constantly to obtain his throne
Always trying to do things on our own
Thinking our thoughts above his own
I can do it all alone
I can be whatever I want
He got it wrong
I ain't missin no ribs
So if I feel this way within
It's got to be right
But not in his sight
Our will
Will never over power his might
Since Eden he's been trying to show us the light
All his children
Adam and Eve alike
He does not hate any of us
No matter how altered we may make ourselves in his sight
He just wants to make us all whole again
Returned to the purified form in which he first imagined
Molded with thoughts and holy hands

From before the creations of any human lands
We all live in this cursed skin
Humanities curse engulfs us all
But Christ was Gods extended hand
To prevent our greatest fall
He begs that we don't spite him
He says he'll forgive all transgressions against him
But how can he move on for you
If you constantly call him a liar
If you say perfection has made a mistake
In your design
How can the created know more than the divine
How can the sinner draw the boundary lines
Of what is right and wrong
He knows beyond our imaginations meager parameters
He knew the thoughts you'd have before you were old enough to have them
He knows all human pain
Sides, Christ was tempted on all of them
He died so over this flesh would could become conquerors
All our feelings overcome
How can he be your God
If you know better than him
He knows you're right when you say
That I just do not fit into this skin
But that's because your body's only human
And all our spirits come under their unique own afflictions
But one can never fully trust in their feelings
Cause human flesh is emotional
But the spirit to his will is submissive
Obedience to him is our purest instinct
He died for all not some
He wants for all his daughters and sons
To his Kingdom come

Trapped...
Engulfed in your smile
You beckon me
Call me in sweet smelling whispers
Your everything calls my name
I just can't seem to turn my face away
You look so gorgeous
Your clothes fit just right
And I know with you
Success is guaranteed tonight
The secrets tattle through your eyes
You shashay in front of me
Masterfully showing off the prize
Got me hipnotized
Floating like a cartoon bubble outside my mind
Telling me to submit to the sublime
Press your lips gently up against mine
And succumb to my addiction
Just one more time

Backslidin

I know we all start on the bottom
But so many slowly raise to the top
Finding strength in your footsteps
Submitting themselves to you
And I did so too
But like so many among the few
I've reached a place where I can't feel u
I say prayers in your name
Set goals for myself in vain
Feel like I'm eroding from all this pain
Falling back into sin once again
Why do I turn away from you
Let this skin lure me into sin
Cleanse myself of filthy mistakes
Only to repeat them over again
Why do I continue this pattern
That destroys my soul within
I've screamed at you
Asked what you want me to do
Like I don't owe my
My everything to you
I know Christ died so of my sin I'm free
So why is it's hold so strong over me
So fleeting seem all my victories
This monster so hard to remove from me
I'm headed toward some terrible tragedy
If I can't overcome this humanity
And stop my backsliding
To elevate my soul to the Christ in me
My brother and sister please pray with me

Afraid Of My Own Shadow

Do you know what it's like to fear
Your own shadow
Mine grows bigger in the dark
So big my footsteps don't seem to fit
Can't seem to slip into the silhouette
That is the real me
Why can't my true talent grow in
The light
Why can't I fight this urge to hide in the darkness
My shadow has encapsulated me
Disabling me to be free
Restraining my talent to my psyche
Where no one gets to see
The true potential of me
The devil laughs triumphantly
As Gods gifts hide internally
Instead of shine ethereally
Like Gods plan for my contribution
To humanity
Instead I cower incessantly
Unable to experience my true artistry
Trapped in my own inadequacy
Scared of my own shadow
Afraid to embrace the light and grow
Condemning mighty words that were meant to inspire
To deflate of all their worth and expire

Pale grays
Make for gloomy days
A shadowy haze
Engulfs my once bright prospects
Will they shine again
Will triumph ink my pen
Will the sun these clouds transcend
Will these harsh times ever end
Cause pale grays
Make for gloomy days
But I wanna live in heavens gaze
Where Gods love warms my face
Where fulfillment and dreams embrace
Where I'm dwelling in Christ's grace
And pale grays don't exist

What's the reason
For the seasons of my misfortune
Karma seems unlikely
So maybe I'm the devils fun
My unhappiness seems the devils project
The demons pastime
The underworlds delight
Their own homely incarnation of torture
In my own little private hell
Where hope gives glimpses
Like little girl teases
But then withholds the true prize
Just at the right time
Using the element of surprise
For my calculated demise
Blissful rest is the mirage in this dessert
It laughingly vanishes as soon as you get close
It's as illusive as my realized hopes
It's unknown to me like the intentions of God
But the devils intentions I know full well
To destroy my entire being and on earth be restricted to his hell
Since my acceptance of Christ has gained my acceptance into heaven
He's seemingly made a vow to till death make me regret it

No one truly sees the pain hidden behind my eyes
Pain so deep it often even seems incurable to the divine
Though in his presence one is supposed to feel sublime
And I personally hate to hear people whine
I too break sometimes
I ain't no jay-z
God I don't claim to be
Wrapped in the same flawed flesh called humanity
Are you and me
Though there lives a God in me
I am not the Deity
I am meant to walk in his authority
But his implanted spirit is only the seed
His immeasurable love gift
For reconnecting to his family tree
But this walk is filled with strugglin
And yes I know I walk with him
But why's my walk so much more troublin
I've always been Mr. nice guy
The suffer through my own stuff while
Makin others smile kind
The positive
Head always held high
The dream real big
Always rise to the top
Gives it his all at everything
Poster boy for through Christ we can do anything
How u doin
I'm fine with a smile guy
Trust in him and encourage others
Against all odds
Stay strong it could always be worse
I'm too proud to cry guy
But I secretly lay awake at night
I sit in silence tryin not to cry
I drink
I brood
I think bad thoughts
I've screamed at God many times
Made thunderous heaven bound cries

Why lord
With how hard I try
How much I put at stake with my own life
As much as I put others first
Why must I dwell in this dimension of otherworldly hurt
Why must I not receive reciprocation of worth
Why can't I experience tranquility
Peace in at least modest calamity
I know u died to save me from sin
And that I needed and accepted you in
And that in itself is the highest blessing
I know In this poem I've said a lot of buts
And I know your sacrifice was more than enough
But it's so hard to stay tough when
You are treated like a foundation
But are hard pressed for stability
When you really need support
I know you made me from the dirt
And often we as humans act as if we regard you with equal worth
But why does Mr. nice guy
Try real hard to be the right guy
Seem to be the one targeted with
Bad lucks biggest bulls eye
Why can't I get a break
Why can't I walk the road of real victory
That spans longer than the shortest distance to the next catastrophe
You know I no longer blame you but
It's hard to summarize a life of unfulfilled dreams
Determined by the strongest of wills
And I know the narrow path is not paved with ease
But
Lord I'm cryin out
Cause I know only you can deliver me

Stars don't need to align
To experience the divine
Just like stars don't spark
The combustion of my pain
But the dreams I have
Do seem to live in stars
Dwelling far beyond my reach
Farther then fulfilling destines
Time hasn't elapsed to moments meant to be
Though they were promised from before the birth of me
When a star signaled his arrival
So why am I strugglin for survival
When will my wish come falling on my star
When will my dreams stop hovering in the sky
Promising my desire
Fading in the will to inspire
They once were consumed with a fire
Determined never to expire
God please give me the power
To keep on reaching higher
Before once extended arms go limp
And my constellation only leads the way to sorrow

Have u ever yearned for more than mediocre
I have
I've never believed
I deserved anything less
The sound of the word
Makes lumps in my chest
Puts gaps in my breaths
I ever only dreamed of success
Since sucking milk from the breast
I developed this concept
That for me it'd always be more
And never less
And I haven't met a person yet
That after talkin
Or seein me do my thing
would ever contest
That I was built to not just graze
But soar above the rest
So explain to me
Why I haven't acheived it
It surely isn't effort
I've dedicated my life to this
How many years of commitment
Does it take to get the proper acknowledgement
Compensation for motivation
Capital to match the talent you hold
Thus fate for all your faith
Cause my destiny is more than mediocre
And the only question I want God to answer
Is how much longer must I wait

Times have gotten so hard
They've even seeped thru to my soul
They're trying to break me
Like weeds their leeching away at my goals
Trying to my willpower implode
To Christ I'm trying to hold on
Cause to the world I'm feeling exposed
My own strengths long since have been engulfed
And most times I feel broken and alone
He's blessed me with a limited few
To count on when troubles fall like dew
But so often they just won't do
That's if they even try to
Cause I'm more of the helper than the helped
I'm never too busy
But scales weigh unbalanced when reciprocity is due
One would guess this would make me cling more to you
But too often I find myself resenting you
Like the spoiled kid who just can't get their way
But it's just not that easy
To a pillar of standards be
When your world seems devoid of proven creeds
Devoid of realized dreams
A chasm of hopelessness
A black hole of wants and needs
I'm a son of the one true king
I thought I inherited prosperity
On earth as well as heaven
I'm no Jew
But I do my best to follow your commandments
So where's my fallen manna
I starve to feel your touch
I wanna believe
Christ I wanna see
But bad luck and misfortune are steady blinding me
I wanna be free
I wanna feel more prayers and less
Complaints are reaching you
I wanna know Gods blessings
More than Satans gloom

I don't know what else to do
But vent these David like psalms
Bind these flowing tears
And press on placing my trust in you

I'm not your superwoman
God that is just one superfluous phrase
That I'd just love to smash through the ground
Of course your not
And I'm no superman
But at least I never infer to be
I know I've got complexities
And sometimes
Dare I say inadequacies
Well pardon me for my humanity
But what do you really want from me
I've given you all my dreams
My hopes my fears my eternity
I already put that ring on your finger
So why are you tryin so hard to talk me down up off this alter
As if life hasn't kicked my ass enough
Why's coming home gotta be as tough
Just one more argument
Just one more complaint
How many unnecessary apologies
Will it take
Before my patience finally breaks
And our love as powerful as it's always been
Due to unrest and lack of peace
Must end
How useless will it be
To be superhuman then

Baby I want you back
I know I did wrong but time
Has been my teacher
And sad songs have been made permanent in my hearts home
Damn I was the fool
Fell victim to the 80 20 rule
Now I'm left with less then 20%
Cause I'm 100% of nothing without u
Whatever I have to do
Just ask and it will be swiftly mastered for u
Cause forget the devils sanctum
I've endured hell since I lost you
It's like I raped happiness
So I could rot inside regret n brokenness' four walls instead
I don't know what I was thinkin
But my hindsight is crystal clear
I'd endure crucifixion type pain
Just to slightly share your world again
I'm a Greek tragedy trying to rewind the times
A discarded poem trying to find the smothered words
An ancient love story trying to mend torn pages
My crying heart yearns to piece back together yours broken pieces
To remove the shadows off once happy memories
Heal the wounds of the ones in between
And lay the foundation for the mantle to rest profoundly happy future
portraits
In the home where our love was redeemed

Her Feet Go Down To Death
Why do you do the things you do
Then run throughout the street cryin' victim
When you are the one
Who injects your venomous poison
Your personality hasn't yet evolved into character
It only further builds your web of deceit
In which you pretend to be kind and caring
A precious gem when in actuality you're a rusty knife
Carnal with only the intent of killing or creating a torturous life
You don't cut low
You don't cut the throat
You don't stab in the back
You flatter your way in with warm embraces
Gentle touches
Warm smiles
Hiding the filthy intentions of an evil spirit
You whisper his name seemingly with passionate love
And when he turns to great you with open arms
He meets your rusty knife
He falls to his knees with tears in his eyes
Starting up in utter disbelief as if betrayed by the divine
As he collapses into a pool of blood without the energy to speak
Massacred by a game of elaborate, brilliant deceit
She snickers, as he is unaware until it is too late
He can only wonder why his precious gem would do him this way
How could his precious gem be a fake
The thoughts seem to parade throughout his mind for eternity
As his stolen life fades away

Because Of Her
Because of her he wakes up with a smile
Because of her his day is worthwhile
Because of her this man has a twinkle in his eye
He has a desire to take his woman higher
Because of her his mind overflows with romantic endeavors
Moonlit dinners, moonlit nights on the beach
Elegant love poems and constant bunches of flowers
To cover her apartment with various fragrances
Because of her he'll tell his boys
It's time to bounce
Because of her
There are countless shopping sprees
With endless bank accounts
Because of her he yearns to succeed
To make his money achieving his childhood dreams
Not hustling on the streets
Because of her he cleans up his life
Doesn't get drunk or get high every night
He isn't perfect but he has excepted
Jesus Christ into his life
Because of her he's a breathtaking sight
He dresses tight and even if he isn't rich
His heart is always right
Because of he he's even happy when he's struggling
He does sometimes get discouraged
But he's never gets defeated because he lives to prosper
For his woman and if he has any his children
Because of her he is him
Imperfect yes, because he's only human
But still always tryin to think
What would Jesus do in this situation
But wait this story isn't over
Because of her it is not the end
Because of her this man is not the end
Because of her this man that makes u go… awww
That man that tugs at hour heart
That man that listening to this
Thoughts of him puts butterflies in your stomach
Because of her that man is… extinct

Because of her that man died an excruciatingly painful death
Because of her he didn't lose his physical life
But instead she killed him by heartbreak
Because of her his heart was broken bit by bit
Into smaller and smaller pieces till no pieces were left
Now all that's left is a void
A dark cold abyss where a heart used to exist
Because of her that man is forced to walk the rest of his days
A heartless, a being void of feelings and emotions
Because of her there is one more man somewhere
Who could care less about anyone but himself
So from now on when you're with a man who truly cares
A man that does all the right things
Says all the right things
A man whose head is together even if his wallet isn't the fattest
A man who calls at least once a day just to say I love you
That man that doesn't argue
That doesn't raise his hand
Who doesn't curse and grunt or whistle at you
That treats you as equal and nothing less
That will go see your movie or do what you want to do instead
That man that will give you that last piece of food
While cuddling after a long day
Don't push him aside
Don't kick him to the curb and holla go get it
Don't persecute him because of his kindness, love, or Christ likeness
Love him right back and never forget
Because of her that man that hits his woman
That man that's pimpin or yellin yo shorty in the street
Might be the same man who was showerin his woman
With love before I began to speak
Oh and just know that she isn't a distant memory
She lives inside each one of you
So leave her locked away and step up and be
A real woman
All she wants for Christmas
Is for him to feel Christ's bliss
Experience his happiness
On the day celebrating his arrival to us
Cause she feels he is finally giving up

She thought that he was stronger
That when she got weak
He could always be her shoulder
She didn't realize he cries tears too
But now his tears are creating wounds
On her soul
Cause she feels the pressure of his goals
She wishes she could take control
Make his dreams bloom like hers are
But she's already carrying the weight of her elevation
Now he's adding his emasculation
And now she's getting closer to breakin
Cause he used to be her stability
Stand tall in all adversity
Hold up the walls that seemed were crumblin
Now he's the one who's fumblin
His complaints out of him keep bubblin
And now she's cryin often when
He's supposed to make her smile
Make her feel divine
Exalted her as his wife
And now she's feeling bad
That Christmas is falling limp on him
Cause even bottomless trees praise the lord from within
Even fake ones shine the lights of him
The one in spite all we all should be praisin when
It's him who gave the ultimate gift
One there's no need to return
Cause he's gonna return
And wipe this world clean from sin
Leaving a world of only sacred kin
Her tears remind her husband of this
He decides to shut his lips
Endure his sufferin like a man without complaint
And lift their Christmas up to the name that lies within

Why

Must she

Be

Constantly... in my head

Why can't I cleanse her memory

Lord would that be heavenly

Cause she keeps tormenting me

Thoughts of her keep tempting me

Regardless of the fact she's

Made it obviously

Clear to me

That my dearest feelings

Fall inadequately

Unable to form reciprocity

Rise back to and beyond the seemingly

Feelings of yesterday

Before I knew true dismay

When our love was masked vicariously

Through familiarity

When my love was locked away

Innocently in my thoughts

Unclouded by advice

Unshunned by the validity

Of the I guess insanity

Of others eyes

Only known by my pen and me

To be an unshakable maybe

But I digress from lately

After secrecy fades

Permission is granted

Opportunity arrives

I try

And what I've perceived truly

For the very first time

Soulmate destiny dies

Like my heart in my hand

Ripped from my chest and

Cried to this page

And yet past lately

To eternity

I still can't dislodge her soul from me
Every once and a while
When I'm fooled into believing I'm free
Though someone said soulmates aren't
Always meant to be
Cause God gave us the inreliquishable
Though obviously swayable choice
Of to be or not to be
Mans question eternally
Of where to be
Visions of her
Invade my innermost psyche
Though I know in my heart she's
Not thinking twice about me
In-spite of how close we used to be
Why

What do you do when husband becomes boyfriend number 2

I cry inside these lines
Because to let these tear flow
Outside these written pages
Would only bring you pain
So I play the man role
I've showed weakness long enough
I let my pen bleed through these words
So self inflicted secrets
Don't clot my heart
Till I can no longer tell what's real
So panic can no longer attack my breathing
Since you became my air
I hold you with arms terrified to let go
Cause you feel like a slippery string
One wind from joining all the other balloons lost in
He blew it skies
Soaring ominously over
She's the one that got away
Memory lanes
But I'm stuck on how can I live without her drive
Trying desperately to make you love me again
While fighting the paralyzing thought I might be just prolonging your
Imminent departure
And I can't even cry
I must draw inside the lines
Give my all to try
And not end up back on heartbreaks door
Cause this time it's more like life break
Like nothing will ever be the same
Where never conquers eternity

Helpless
Cause I can't say a word
But there's no silence in my head
No warmth within my bed
My soul can never rest
I want you back
I want our love intact
You say you want to work for the same
But your standing even further away
I know I caused you pain
But not this way
No wound festers more deep
Then forced trust in instability
Reliance on justified insecurity
But it's exactly what you need
You can't stand to hurt me
But this further tortures your necessity
I gave you everything you asked for
I gave more than all of me
Righted every wrong
You acknowledge
Then kill all chances of consistency
You made your points clear but you don't want them proven right now
They're too overwhelming
But what about me
Loves not selfish
But where's my reciprocity
My right to any lasting dignity
Have I not endured enough calamity
Forgiven enough insanity
How are you the only victim
When I've so many knives driven in my back
Yet I still gaze lovingly waiting to meet
Eyes explored by someone else
Lust soaked lips
And a ravished heart
And what do I have to show for it
...I don't know

Your Love Only

You're the one I want
And no one else
If I can't have you
Then I'll stay lonely by myself
If love is not your love
Love just isn't worth havin
I'd rather be reminiscin
Then in the arms of someone different
All I do is think about you
Waiting for your call
And when you don't call I get depressed
But I call you anyway
Even though you don't make the effort yourself
I can't seem to put the thought of your love
Out of my mind
So I walk around aimlessly
Eternally lonely
And to anyone else's love, blind

I stand behind her in the mirror
And I see flawless beauty staring back at me
Naked perfection
Unabashed and unashamed
But I'm aware of the scars on her heart that lie beneath
I wish my lips could kiss through to the hurt
Reach so deep down on your skin
They could touch upon your scars n alleviate the pain like a loved one
Kissing a child where it hurts
Only I'm the one that caused the pain
Who could never diminish flawless beauty
But could very well let her slip away
So I take in her essence as I stand behind her in the mirror
I hold her gently to remember where she fits so perfect
And regardless if it's too late
I tell her of her worth to me
Just so she knows I know it's true

Happiest when we were all alone
When nothing stood in our way
When it was just us vs. the world
Those nights in the dorm when we would just talk then make love
Rest your head in my chest and then fall asleep to each others
adorations with the sounds of music or t.v. on low in the background
Then as I'd start to leave you'd beckon me back to bed for one last goodbye
And after I was gone you'd sit at home and gain pleasure from thinking of our
next embraces
Happiest when we were alone
In that basement apartment cemented in dreams of bigger and better things
We overcame floods and bad conditions
With prayer and love
Your screams bounced of the tiny walls
Until they transcended to other floors
Our love would dwell in many rooms of that house
But we were happiest when we were alone
Free from the distractions others brought from their worlds
Regardless of good or bad
It was no longer just us against the world
We no longer clung to each other always
But were surrounded by other things as well
Your screams got dimmer but my overexposed ears could not tell the
difference
Affections grew more private to hide from others eyes
Our love stripped of its freedom
And we unknowingly bore those scars
Then we finally broke away
We did the things we always wanted to do
We went places we could not go before
We were able to adore each other fully in more than just one room
And though at times we'd argue
We'd rest in each other and bring us through
But then our world became crowded again
Trails and tribulations to me you could not truly vent
Once again others stood in our way
Regardless of the rights or wrongs left in their wake
Your soul yearned for private like time
And it deserved not to have it feel it could keep momentarily drifting
away

But every time we'd start to get close there's another interruption
And in this cycle of constant imposed restrictions
We each at different times would put others before ourselves
Thus steadily losing more of us
It had been so long we forgot the difference
Were deaf to privacy's desperate cries for attention
Either way a darkened road disguised the distance
Created by your steadily hardening heart
But now the hidden roads been lit by another
And this distraction is the greatest to date
He's the filler of all my shortcomings
The fulfiller of the needs I've not met
A distraction from all the distractions already set
They're gone now but it's hard to see that cause the stage has already
been set
And now it's so hard to reject the idea of seeing how things play out
I see I've disappointed so deep your afraid to trust me again
I now see the devastation of these distractions
More importantly how things have pulled us away from our anchor in all
storms within
I gave up the man role and lost our grounding from sin
Now Christ is ragin within
But I'm so far away with you traveling the opposite direction I don't
know if I can make it
I've been drivin runnin hitchin
But I can't seem to make it back to you
I keep stumbling on traps
Inadvertently setting myself back
Tryin so whole heartedly to just get back
When we were happiest all alone
Where our bed was filled with unabashed moans
Our lives cemented in the will to overcome
Our dreams tied in destiny to become
Doing all the things we planned to do
Seeing all the things we planned to see
Adding to the adventures we've already experienced
Together
When we completed each others thoughts, aspirations, and dreams
Together
Envisioned, already in flight

Our desires and our needs
The raising of our seed
We were always happiest when we were all alone just you n me
Just us vs. the world

Have u ever experienced true agony
It's wrapped in nothingness
Feeling of seeming invisibility
That burns through the skin of your heart
You know you're there
But u know your not
Till your stomach knots
Trying to get comprehension
To your brain
Trying to get you to refrain
From loneliness going insane
Cause you just can't cleanse them from your mind
Stop the constant rewind
To days you were by their side
Days you were blessed to behold their smile
Be the cause of their laughter
Free of the hell of this hereafter
The agony
Of knowing they're not in a better place
Not dead
Just forever out of the reach of your embrace
By some bonds unknown to you
Some shame or disgrace
Your unconditional love can't retrace
So you just wallow in the grief
Of your disbelief
Broken in unrivaled undeserved
Agony
Praying to be free of their memory
Yet praying for them to embrace your memories
So you can renter their life
And build new memories
But your not on their friends list
Your face doesn't reside in her pics
Your shelved with the floppy disks
Stored with the irrelevant memories
Devoid of the realm of their happiness
Where in younger days you'd always exist
But in these present days
Only agony persists

Feedin on the tears you bear at the look

Or remembrance of every moment poem or sight of new or old pic

Trapped in this skin that burns eternal

Right through to the pores of your heart

Till it pores put through thick blood

Fusing through now thickened skin

Isolated into emotional nothin

Alone to face the inner torturin

Of heartbroken soulstruken

Agony

I look back through my old poetry books
And all I wanna do is smile
Let out reminiscent sighs
Of older days
And different times
The growing me sprinkled through emphatic lines
Character building
Historical primes
But I can't
Cause all I see is pages of heartache
And turmoil
Of my tortured feelings for you
Other poems only seem to fill the blanks
In the devastating annals of the history of you
And all the unrequited love of me
The prologues of friendship
The tales of tragic misconceptions
Followed by the sequels of hurt and betrayal
The volumes of separation and insurmountable love that logic would
reason should have turned to hate
The seemingly indiscernible by you Catalogue of pain and torture of
the loss of everything that was us
So much deeper than the lust others showed you yet you seemed instead
to trust
Completed by the inevitable acceptance that not all soulmates are
meant to be
The forgiveness only possible since
Christ gave wife to grant true levity
But you still haunt these pages
Like the ghost of true loves past
Yet not like the other great loves that accentuate their pages
And transition into art that might one day inspire the masses to smile
And dream of love
Your presence doesn't come off so transparent
Doesn't seem so distant in the abyss
Of yesteryear bliss
With long gone first kisses
And maybe she'll be the one
Misses

Reading it's tortured pages
Still has a sting that's transcended through the ages
And so
Though my poetical legacy has so much more stowed away within it's
history
The temptation to destroy my past when reading these books is eatin me
Though the connection we had was infinitely deeper than the now
traumatic memory
The knowing it obviously didn't mean as much to she
Since even before words died between us
We no longer shared each others company
And if asked about those times she barely remembers anything
Our tale could never be less then legendary
So I just close those books
Return them carefully from whence they came
And I pick up my pen
To continue to write new stories
Of now barely an associate
Probably never again close friend
But whole
No longer broken

Independent darkness
Trying to get used to the idea of doing me for me
It's hard when your so used to putting someone else first
Sleeping on another side of a once full bed
Feeling empty
With nothing to touch your soul
But sweet made bitter memories
Remembering the hours lost watching them sleep
Always putting your self at peace
Now easy days seem to run on forever
Sprinting as fast as u can
Taking as few breaths as possible
To outrun your marathon thoughts
Of why's
How comes
And I just want you yesterdays
Making sharp stabs by the non dream reality that is today
Fast with disaster the devil is
And your head is spinnin wonderin
How'd I get here
Left to be held by only me
With only Gods love keeping u from
Ending everything

Ma
I'm not trying to bore you
Wit no simple introduction
No hood game
No manufactured formal smoothness
All those words would just fall banal
At the feet of your obvious beauty
What can I say that you haven't already heard
What could describe that won't come off as mediocre or sub par
To reach beyond just a scratch of the surface
Of your unexplainable transcendence of beauty
that would leave the truest player without even one smooth word to speak
My swag ain't worth the streets it glided down
With you standing right before me
Me stuck at ma
Cause I ain't been this at loss for words since birth
So I just repeat it ma
With this as the first of infinite love poems that somehow become
finite as they instantly parade their multitudes swiftly yet memorably
through my brain
And I say
Ma I'm left speechless but I know I need to know your name
And maybe over near future days I can slowly reveal all the poems of ode
to all that is you
That just in this moment in time and space
Were forever
Engraved into my brain

New Love

You ever been around a girl so fine
You try not to fix your eyes
On her undeniable gorgeousness
Cause you know that just one look won't be enough
Once you meet her gaze you might never be able to avert your sight
from her frame again
You can discern her voice from a mile away
It's like a symphony to your ears
Only Beethoven couldn't even find her notes in his greatest years
Her presence evokes your most intense fears
Cause you're paralyzed with fear at the thought of losing her
Thus why your too scared to even take it there
But she's so perfect
Cowardice would only result in deep regret
I mean she's so beautiful even when your eyes are closed
Her beauty your mind can't forget
It's like heaven hasn't even realized
Their angel of beauty left yet
Cause she's right here next to me
Even lowered eyes can see
Lord knows unspoken poems do scream
At me to let them be
But I'm bound by insecurity
Though I get to be in proximity
To a girl that's essence begs to question
If God is not a woman
Cause her love is supernatural
I want her in my heart
And I want to be in hers
I wanna worship in her temple
And give her glory on my knees
While she supplies all of my needs
Cause I give her my everything
She far outshines the dime
With the ridges of her quarter
She's the type of girl that gets playas
To plan for sons and daughters
Rings are the thoughts on the minds of those that engage her
Married to more than her physical is the spirit of all those fortunate

enough to meet her
But I just need to tell her
That her beauty has eclipsed my world
And I've been too overwhelmed to pull my hands from my eyes
And peer bravely into the rare antiquity of her future

Unconditional Love
In a world where so much is going wrong
I thank God everyday for a love going strong
Despite the most trying times we press on
Wrapped in Christ's sacred union
I always wake up to glorious sunsets
Cause next to me my sun rests
I lay next to my precious light
That continually brightens my nights
Enhances my days
With her love that's so amazing
It's everlasting
It's counteracting
It's abounding
And it's never ending
Cause nothing else is an option
We choose to love above all things
Love above any arguments
Disappointments obstacles or frustrations
To her I pledge my allegiance
Despite our mistakes
Despite our flaws
In her is my hearts home
Our love is etched in stone
Her beauty exclaims its name
Our love cannot be tamed
Will never be maimed
In my life she will always remain
Because of her... Loves first sight to eternity
My life will never be the same
In the way of cheesy fairy tales
Legends of old that travail
The epic stretches of time
In which histories intertwine
And only the truest destiny's survive
Into the minds and hearts of future generations
Despite the limitations
Of our fragile emotionality
Our love Christ built eternally
Cause we laid our love down at his feet

And he washed us with his blessings
Saying she was made by him just for me
And I'll live my whole life thanking him
As we continue to build
From now until eternity

I thought that you should know

One may ask me do you love her
But that would be a foolish question
One could ask do you show it
And I would answer I believe I do
But the key is to never be fully comfortable
To always let them know
So I just want to tell you how I feel
I love you and you are my world
You keep me strong and always maintain my confidence
I can always be myself, no games, no acting, when I'm with you
When I doubt myself you're always there to encourage me
To say you love me, kiss me, and tell me "Baby you can do anything"
You're my joy, my peace, my very best friend
Whenever I need to talk you always listen
When everyone else is nowhere to be found
We're honest with each other when we're happy
When we're sad
When we're wrong
When we're uncomfortable
And even when we're afraid the other will be mad
We hold no punches and that's what makes our loves so strong
You are my center, you complete the puzzle that is me
You never try and separate Jesus from my heart
Instead you openly greet him with open arms and he embraces you
Making our love protected in his shield of love and mercy
If everyone were to turn their backs on me today
I know you would still be by my side
Because you love me for me, not the external but what's inside
And I love you the same with all my heart
Christ is my foundation and you are my center
As my love and my very best friend

Where I Wanna Be

As day turns into night I sometimes get scared
That the next morning I might be gone without you near
What kind of world would that be
Not the kind of world I ever want to see
Now that you are mine
I never want to return to old times
I don't wanna reminisce
On my old life filled with bliss
I never again want to live in the darkness
Of that solar eclipse of loneliness
In which you didn't exist
I just want to rejoice
In the heat of the unobstructed sun
Bask in the glow of the heavenly angel
Who came from above to be with me
For today, tomorrow
And every other moment
From now until eternity

Who Needs Dreams

I lay awake and stare
At her half naked silhouette
In the moonlight and smile
With pride
That not even the night
Can shadow the light
Of my sight
Of true love
That emanates from her every curve
Cultivates in her spirit
And reveals it's treasures in her
Actions and words
I love to watch her like this
Asleep
At peace
Knowing she can always rest assured
I can lose a minute of rest or two because
Her love exceeds my dreams

She is completion
Fulfilling my unfinished masterpiece
She is the key
To the kingdom of my forever
The door to the palace of my prosperity
She is the rock
That stands like an immovable beam
To support through natural disasters
She's the rain
That sashes down my window pane
Putting me in that tranquil poetry mood
That aphrodisiac
To my sexual chocolate groove
The star
That accentuates my world
Her essence her style her soul
Are the planets
That make my galaxy
The envy of the universe
She's the victories in my success
She's the diamond in the rough
She's the breakthrough moments
In my illustrious career
She's even the ying to my yang
Balancing out my thoughts
So they can make it to a page
That's sings love songs
To her name
While she gives Christ all the honor and the praise
Cause it's he that made us this way
Preparing her for me
With his unfathomable attention to detail
Making her perfect for me
In his love before he even gave time a thought
That's why we'll never be apart
Unless God makes time restart
In which instance we'll start all over again
Like clichés of
Happily ever end
Like romantic comedies

Where lovers evolve from friends
And cheaters never win
And a marriage is the final scene
And a man calls his woman his queen
Or says without you there's no me
Or your kiss is so heavenly
Cause you were sent by heavens king
And unlike men who get that rib back and act like they never really
needed it
I wear this ring as a symbol of its necessity
And I won't stop letting you know how much I love you
Cause he ordained us to loves eternity

Spoken Word Poem To You
I open my eyes
And look to the other side
Of me
And I see
The other side of me
And that is you
And my mind starts to reel
Thinking of what to say
What words can grace my page
To speak to all that is you
And it's evident
That this morning I am compelled
To write a spoken word poem about you
Those things that you do
To make me… crazy
You be sendin me in dazes
Yet I keep wantin to send you daises
Cause your simply amazin'
From your searching eyes
That pierce thru mine to my soul
Encouragin all my goals
Building me when I wanna fold
Your duty is to continually reshape the mold
That God has made into ribless me
You are the key
Often to my insanity
But more importantly
Into the complete me
Cause no matter how angry you make me
I am yours
And you are mine
Our destinies are eternally inclined
To be intertwined
Like the story of Christ and I
And Christ in you
Cause God has brought one together from two
He ordained me to you
You are more than just my boo
You're my wife

My eternal life
Will be spent in love with you
And every thing I do
Will be infused with the glory of you
Only you can make me fume
Wanna yell, scream, kick, and storm out the room
But when facing impending doom
I wanna suffer the storm
Trapped in the open or behind closed doors with only you
Cause you're the one I wanna hold under the moon
The sunset I want to offset my manana, evening, and noon
Just spoon under the stars
Make sweet love to you while songs accented by acoustic guitars
Play in the background
I want that track playing on repeat round
Till you can't distinguish between the sound
Of that passionate R+B groove
To the shaking of our bedroom
And it's screams
Of heavenly ecstasy
In which exists only you and me
Under the sanctity of our covenant
Under the now valley of our covers
Into the screams of our pillows and bed
In time that seems to never end
Cause you are the girl who whispered through my dreams
God's promise since before my teens
Since before I could comprehend my vital needs
Since before the creation of the heavens and the earth and the conception to God of Eternity
He thought of giving you to me
And I'll spend the rest of my days thanking him
No matter how many times you make me say things I think are right are wrong
No matter how many times you drive me to drink or punch a wall
That will never outweigh the day I stood at that alter with tears of joy
In my eyes as my dove, my partner for life
Walked down that aisle
Under the watchful eyes of God
The gaze of my friends and family
Prayed into the covenant by our pastor
And our souls bonded into oneness by the holy spirit

I know with super human certainty
That I wanna spend eternity
Living in one accord with the day I imagined since we met
Whose beat played from my heart in which it rests
To the page, thru my lips, on this stage
In an unsilencible spoken word poem to you

Unbreakable
While you hate
Try to Tear down and break
I stand strong unbreakable in God
My spirit burns too bright
Your temporary pain can't blow out
The fire burning inside
That determining drive
That Jesus Christ ignites
God sheds truth on your deceit
Me, you can never defeat
Your evil will never gain the victory
I may sometimes get discouraged
But I never give up the fight
You're dreaming if you ever think
You'll win
When that happens
Jesus will sin

How laughable that we won't believe in Jesus
But we can believe in what we see
Though since ancient past years
We see the things of this world disappear
We've even worshipped statues whole heartedly
Made so obviously from rock and stone
But we put bloody to the cross Jehovah
Hold on
This makes no sense we put our faith in the untrustworthy
Like a man or a woman has ever obtained full purity
A total blameless life for a man is a blatant impossibility
That's like snakes standing upright since the serpent tempted Adam and
eve
You Wont worship him
You wanna steal Gods glory
Soundin like Lucifer before the fall
Thinkin your capable of it all
But when has a man ever escaped
Deaths judgment
You can continue to call
Man, me I'm the one in control
But in the afterlife
Heaven or Hell
Is ultimately His call
And you don't have to believe me
He gave you the choice to live your life
As you will to
But I'll surrender my all to his will
So in the end to his victory I'll be entitled
And I don't mean like rappers thanking God for what I do on this mike
I mean surrender my gifts talents
My all
Surrender my life
Cause he is the light at the end of the tunnel
Without him the ball I would constantly fumble
But he's the rock
That supports my dreams
Keeps me healthy on my feet
And supplies my needs
He's the light

The truth
The way
Supreme king
He's Yahweh
The only way
The trinity
The creator of all things
And you can trust in him
Or you can trust in you
But I know the truth
By the world I won't be fooled
He's my lord and savior
And despite my faults my humanity I'll continue to claim him
Cause no matter what you say to or about me
He's the only one who can save men
So despite today's cries of tolerance for anything imma give him the
glory
So in the book of life he'll write my name and my story

If God gave you the skills and said that you'd be one of the greatest
But u gotta trust in me and always be patient
How long would it be before you gave up
Before you gave in
Cause his timings not like yours
And it seems like you'll never win
And you're continually fallin back into sin
And you feel like he's never gonna allow you true victory
Till you can stop fallin back into travesties
But you know you can never be heavenly
Cause your always gonna be part of humanity
So u lose faith cause it's been so long losing
So many hopes been lifted up just to get crushed to the ground
Feelin like your only crown is the clown one
Thought he said the battles already won
But all your left is doubtin them
His promises
Seeming so reach less
Regardless of the given talents
And that's just how a brutha feels
But I know he doesn't welch on deals
So how am I gonna up my faith resolve
And get on one accord with the lord
Cause I'm supposed to be his chosen one
And transform my talents to please the son
Jesus Christ died for my sins
So for him I'm not allowed to lose
So I gotta win
Wage the war properly so those who sin
Can't claim to steal his glory in the end

You suck
You have no skill
Your garbage
You'll never succeed
Several phrases that propelled me to victory on these streets
With opponents lining up against me
I further built my prosperity
Cause I'd let no one get the best of me
Who is he or she
To tell me what I can or can't be
Nothin not even infirmities
Would allow me to accept defeat
Cause my Gods promises and
My will power make me incapable
Of giving up or giving in
For me to bow down to mans
Conceptions of me is the greatest sin
Cause the holy spirit of the almighty God resides within
So no matter if I started from scratch
I taught myself
Locked in
And put in the work to learn then excel
Then win
Play like a king
Never back down to a challenge
Give my all
Bring my heart
My soul
My integrity to the court
You can continue to taunt, hate, or scoff
But you're the one working so hard to beat me
And I just wanna ball

Have you ever felt like you can't go on
Your all broken like some old sad blues song
I know those types of times all too well
But I know Gods purpose better
And the drive he's built in me that can't be crushed
Believe, the devil tries
But I strive
Through all the storms and trails
Underailable
I eat blows to the face
With the infinite healer at my side
Pushin me from the inside
Where all my talents reside
Coincide
With the unbreakable spirit
Renewed along with my mind
When I dedicated my life to him
When I submitted my heart to his glory
Mighty he made me
To stand the tests of the world
And those who serve its master
Cause in the end victory can only be his
Cause he paid the price for sin
That we could always win
If we place our trust in him
Claiming our rights as his holy kin
So if you thought that rainy days
Could ever break my stride
That I'd ever concede to no longer try
You must of lost your mind
Cause I'll always overcome, survive
Cause Christ glory
Is the mission of my life
And my tribute is the mastery
Of the talents he provides
That sustain his purpose for my time

I write poetry
So yall can feel me
I divulge my soul
So yall can hear me
I don't shout and scream
Like the poets I see on tv
I don't get a lot of ohs n ahs
People don't tend to stop me with
Random outbursts
Aww shoots
Whoas
No he didnts
Hands crashing tables with banging
Feet crashing floors
Standing ovations
But I write
I write what's inside me
Breathin to escape within
Creep out on my phrases and fragments
On poetic license landings
Hysterical or tragic founding's
Adversities over bounding
I write
To expel my surroundings
I write to draw you in
I write down my purpose
On paper with pens
Spoken words I try to attempt

Spoken Words
Who do I have to be
Who do I have to see
What do I have to do
I experience the glory of you
What words must I say
What graces must I sway
What price must I pay
To bask in the beauty you portray
What contender must I fight
What masterpieces must I write
What wrongs must I right
To continue to hold your sight
What odes must I sing
What treasure must I bring
Over what heights must I spring
For your finger to wear my ring
What journeys must I travel
What prayers must I grovel
What skeletons must I unshovel
To learn the truths amatuers have disheveled
I try to eloquate
But your essence is beyond
My limited words
I try to learn
But your wisdom
Is beyond my understanding
I try to write of you
I try to speak on you
I stand on stages
Trying to preach of you
But I can only scratch the surface of you
So I just keep payin homage to you
Spoken word poetry... Kreativity

People always say cliché things like...
Ya gotta see the big picture
But I've learned the small pictures
Can sometimes add up to a big one
If you just open your eyes
I lived blind for so long
Till Christ did an old school miracle
And restored sight to my mind
Opening blind eyes
Which in turn unmuted the voice
Of my enslaved inner divine
I spoke in the past unleashing
Stuttering vocals groping in the dark
For the truth
Which was in me
I cried out for it but didn't wanna see
It in non HD
I shunned the analog for the 1080p
Which in actuality was the one filled with unclarity
Because God reveals his secrets in mysteries unveiled in a realm outside
Of the worlds "humanity"
He works in the spirit
My Christianity was partial
I thought I'd been seeking
But my spirit grew up behind
Now I'm caught up
Replaying all the little things
The small pictures
Which in the past where blurred
By my teary tragedies
With Gods victories glossing
Over my existence
Like opaque ghosts of important virtues
But Christ shed his blood
For the ultimate victory
He only wanted greatness for me
But I wasn't even grateful for the little things
So what made me think I deserved greater
Then he became the strength in my weakness
Making me whole again

Clearing my vision on the small things
Which I now see were the building blocks
The pieces of the puzzle
That now blend into his portrait of me
Made amazing in the revelation of him

With this pen I used to write my tears
Enlarge all my fears
Voice all my complaints
Unleash all my restraints
But now I submit this pen to him
I use it to worship him
To usher up my prayers
To petition for my brothers and sisters
To minister to my listeners
To glorify his name
My pen still knows of pain and suffering
But my pen is born again
Washed in the ink
Cleansed from sin
Free from proclamations of despair
My pen lives in the victory of Calvary
Boasting of joy and glory
My pen spills compassion and love
Exudes grace integrity and prosperity
My pen speaks of courage and character
My pen writes unmovable unashamed
Of the one who bestows the gifts of all who choose to wield it's
mighty power
Across a page and onto a stage
Jesus

Am I all I say I am
Is this an act or am I for real
You tell me
You let me know the deal
No!
Don't say Nothin!
I'll let you know
I can't afford to pretend
Cause my reality ain't enough
If my passion for this craft could be turned into sunlight
Everything in this universe would be disintegrated under their intense heat
And the sunlight of my passion would burn alone unchallenged
Making the actual sun appear as small as the furthest star
I'm not like someone who has his career handed down
I'm not some rich guy who can afford whatever it takes
Money is no object
But I would sell everything I have minus Jesus, love, my morals, integrity, and soul
To make it in this game
Its not just simply for women, money, and fame
It's more than just a dream
It's my life
My five talents I die each die a painful death
To make ten
My example that there is a God inside of me
It's not just some luxury
I want or desire
It's a goal I need to achieve
You might ask
Am I all I say I am
Well, I cannot afford not to be

People tend to think that only girls are diamonds
But I've got a testimony that's been refined through the fire
So I'd be reminded to lift Jesus higher
When days got dim
I got upset with him
I Let myself feel abandoned
Depressed and broken
Hurt enough to ignore sacrifices given
But what about this air I'm breathin
This warm place where I'm sleepin
This not always abundant
But constant food that I'm eatin
The needs he's frequently meetin
While I'm steady complainin
Mistakes I'm consistently makin
Sin I'm weakly contemplatin
Yeah he's watching my heart breakin
By sequences of crappy situations
Deceptions crumbling through once thought steady foundations
Me trying to positively impact a morally bankrupted generation
Where much more than the economy is in a recession
And I am humbled
That he still loves me
Devotes all of him to save me
Even allow the crucifixion of the deity
The son of the holy trinity
For one who's so unworthy
So though my soul heaves
From the pain hard times have let seep in
He's replaced all my weaks with strengths
Gives me the will to fight again
Stand on his words in the end
As a story of the testimony of him
So though hard times seeped through to my soul
You'll know he's redeemed me as his kin
When over sin and death he got the win
And secured heaven as my eternities end